FEATHERED  GLORY

Poems by Peter Hargitai

Acknowledgments: These poems have appeared in the following publications, to which grateful acknowledgement is made: *College English, Spirit, Blue Unicorn, The Carrel, The Cornfield Review, Palmetto Press, The South Florida Poetry Review, National Poetry Anthology, Dark Tower, Prairie Schooner, Kansas Quarterly, The Apalachee Quarterly, Polyphony, Vox, Isle of Flowers, The Café Review.* Portions of "On Carol Dameron's *The Teacher*" first appeared as "Brueghel's Icarus, for Instance" in *Dark Tower*; "Uncommon Cold" appeared in *Budapest Tales* in 2009. "The Art of Taxidermy," in *College English*, "Cats" in *Isle of Flowers*. "An Owl for Larry Donovan" first appeared in *The Café Review*. "Opening at Town Shores," "Gulfport Morning," "Get Well Card," "Prospecting From Our Window," "Gulfport Pier," "Selfie at Seventy on Face Book," "Anniversary at Bok Tower," "On Carol Dameron's *The Teacher*," "Hallmark Card No. 1," "Hallmark Card No. 2," "Yes I Am Gulfportian" first appeared in the Yellow Jacket Review in 2019.

Contents

FEATHERED GLORY

She saw no swans in her village
The closest was a gaggle of geese
Leaving wedge shapes in dust
Before tottering on cobblestone

But once she was old enough
She got to see one close up
Too close for her own good

Her mother was prying open
A yellow beak as far as it would go
Stuffing fistfuls of cornmeal
Down an airless gullet
That bulged in fits and starts

She never got to learn the art
Of feeding birds without pain
To wheedle grace out of agony
To plant knees on wings and
Twist the neck into an arch
Then a flash of knife
In a sudden stroke
In a gust of wind
She died

Her mother fell over and died
They told her it was the wind
It was the wind that hit her
And she died

She got to learn another art
How to conspire against
The wheels of time
The eyes still and open wide
Little specks on colored orbs
By the corners tiny butterflies

She shakes her and they shatter
Tiny shards into stained glass
The leaden eyes hold them in
Entombed in dust-free oblivion

She props up her feathered glory
The raven hair tousled to the sky
A swan neck embroidered in lace
Like that picture in her other life

In Saint Mark's square
With her dark fascist gondolier
With her outrageous hat and hair
Midnight dances under chandeliers

But all that was in Venice
Before the communists

JANUARY 6, 2021

They came in daylight
The Confederate undead
Swarming out of their
Caves by the thousands
This time as Proud Boys
Boogaloo and QAnon
White supremacists
Tattoed skinheads
With flags and slogans
Tongue-sure and wicked
And armed with guns

Like locusts they storm
Capitol Hill for the rapture
The selfies and the race
And once again
Darkness is made

The demigod of chaos
Incites a lynch mob
To invade the House
And singe their souls
To do the unspeakable
Drag out a man in blue
Beat him half to death
With the stars and stripes

All for the great Baal

The witchunt breaches
Doors and moves inside
Heave ho heave ho
The mob crushes a cop
Into a vise of glass doors
Men in cemo and tactical gear
Look to hang Mike Pence
Burn Nancy at the stake

It is a carnival of hate

A painted QAnon shaman
Bedecked with fur and horns
Sits in the Speaker's Chair
A man flourishes a rebel flag
Another a cluster of zip ties
A bearded man's T-shirt says:
"Camp Auschwitz"

A confederacy of dunces
Live-stream ignorance:
"Hey let's vote on some shit!"

There is a noose and handcuffs:
"Kill him with his own gun!"

They rifle through drawers
A pose in Speaker Pelosi's office
A boot on her desk and a note
Texts and photo after photo:
"I'm in the Capitol lol."

They bash in a cop's head
With a fire extinguisher
Three more die outside
A woman whose flag says
"Don't Tread On Me"
Is trampled to death
By the angry mob

Help arrives way too late
Not a soul arrested inside

Out come the Boogaloo
Escorted by co-conspirators
Fanfare of yelps and yahoos
More selfies with booty
A manic interview or two
Uploading *pat(riots)*
In the twilight's
Last gleaming

Outside the lit dome
There is still no light
Only mourning

And the locusts reenact
Their murderous chorus
In the shadows of the web
Where darkness is made

UNCOMMON COLD

When I have a cold
It is like déjà vu
And I am deceived
I am once again
In the neo-gothic
Immaculate
Conception
Except it is you
That I conceive

Through the alchemy
Of memory and Flonase
Nasal spray
An inexplicable lilac
River of desire
Floods my sinuses
And fills the emptiness

Ah Budapest
It is you that I breathe
And for a moment
Nothing is lacking

The air is delicate
But uncommonly cold
The rarefied oxygen
In bullet-riddled spires
Not carved out of stone

But hacked out of bone-
Splintering longing

On Castle Hill
There is more beauty
In a dome in ruins
Than its bland restoring
More glory in a statue
Remaining headless
Anonymous

A lost relic on a hill of bone

Who is the grand sculptor
Who let the bombs fall
The bullets fly
Chip bone
Freeze blood
Shiver stone
Into frost-fine
Filigree?

Cathedrals of illusion
Snow onto the rubble

Where are you
My Budapest?
Is it always this cold?
A snowflake
Momentary only
Elaborate embroidery
Meant to be destroyed?

BREATHING ON THE VENTILLATOR

I breathe for her.
She is dying of Covid
She is dying hard.
They won't let me in.
I pedal all the way to Palms
To stand outside, bead words
To make amends, fragments
Of light and dark, cloud and sun,
A belated elegy on the bay.

I pant to the congested causeway,
Sighs behind a gleaming line of cars,
Accusing vestiges of unwritten poems:
Scintillating REMs of life, spokes
Of flaking chrome and aluminum.

The drawbridge holds me
But I can't hold her as she dies
No one close will close her eyes
Her ashen mouth still open wide.

A distant ship's horn
Macaws shrieking in vein
A draw bridge tolling
Her passing ark
And all our covenants
To quell that dark.

ON CAROL DAMERON'S THE TEACHER

(oil on wood 48" by 48")

She will never escape the scorched earth
Or sand snaking with oil
Let her mix with clay and ashen rust
To begin her journey on canvas
As desolate as a blinding flash

Let the canyon remain alien
And she the last of the shipwrecked
Her clipped wing accusing
The inhuman landscape

The master painter
Towering above her
Told her too late
To beware of flying
Too close to the sun

The solar wind already melted
The top layer of skin
And severed an arm
From the child body

The doll-like mannequin
Top heavy with a woman's head
Destined to fall end over end

A *salto fatale* into the sea

Will she hit the water without a splash?
Sink into oblivion
With her name written in water?
Will *The Teacher*
Survive her
And live on?

Her life had been
The doldrums
Schoolroom after schoolroom
Keeping a duck or two in tow
Teaching the unteachable
Just when she was about
To reach the unreachable

More than mere woman
Half-child and androgynous
Perhaps a genius
She insisted
On being measured
By her nearness to the sun

She worked that pygmy wing
In exquisite defiance
Enraged the strokes
In lunatic and linseed trances
Prying clawing
Cutting into canvas
To lose herself in it
A last mad *danse macabre*
Her palette sharp and flailing

Maimed but unyielding
Her phantom limb hanging on

But as the body wingéd body
Knifed toward the crawling sea
A cruel glint of sun
Ignited the tiniest of wings
Singeing scarlet
A tinge of orange
Her final act aflame with brilliance
So unlike her subtle masters
So unlike Brueghel's *Icarus*
For instance

PROSPECTING FROM OUR WINDOW

First thing in the morning my wife
Looks for fish in our finger of water
She's known to catch
Prehistoric tarpon scales
Turn into gold in an arc of sun

I watch the sky and see
A falcon hover high above the water
It's a buzzard she says
And then a sharp veer
Flashes its golden keel

More like burnt orange she says
Something's dead
So don't go making a falcon out of it
I tell her I know
As I know that in Florida
Leaves turning yellow are pollen

My falcon-turned-buzzard climbs
Higher and higher in widening circles
There it is again
Definitely golden
Glowing more intense
As it soars westward
And leaves a trail of incandescence

There you go again she says
I am at it again

In fulfillment of my secret legacy
To pole the dead across water
And release their spirit
Only to catch them in flight again

I do this with my arthritic cane
The one leaning against its shadow
The famous walking stick
My father used to tour the continent
A single copper mount
Still boasts of his travels
Hallstatt
A day trip to Austria

That traveler father of yours
Never ventured far from home
My mother said
The myth exploded
When the windshield blew up
In his face when he drove
Head on into an oak
In North Olmsted Ohio
Not even a mile from home

My great falcon had flown

The body buried
In the non-Catholic section
Of Holy Cross Cemetery
With his enormous degree
A diploma all in Latin
About the size of a window
Rolled into a scroll

To fit into his high gloss
Coffin with the copper fittings

—Juris Doctor—

I was told
He never got to use it
Because he was not a realist
Because Hungary lost the war
Because of Communism
Because of his English
Because in America
He was too old
To learn a new legal system
My mother said she had married him
Because she thought he was a good catch
With prospects
As good as gold

HERA AND THE PEACOCK

She adorns his tail with eyes
And he turns to her again,
Aware of the power of images.
Should he raise his plumes
The stiff feathers
Dig in like arrows. The wings

Must drop.
And the dazzling fan spread
Into a whisper of maracas
ornate and gaudy
like ah's
while she holds his quiver.

MOTHER'S A RACIST

My mother's a racist,
She washes the dishes.
My mother's a racist,
She whitens the laundry.
My mother's a racist,
She watches Bill Cosby.
My mother says black lips are ugly.
My mother hates black kinky hair.
My mother hates mothers on welfare.
My mother hates blacks who breed.
My mother hates the air they breathe.
My mother hates the food they eat.
My mother hates soul food.
My mother hates dreadlocks.
On MLK Boulevard she presses the locks.
My mother pairs my socks.
My mother's a racist pure and white.
She spreads her white tablecloth
For an ethnic picnic. Her hate runneth over.
My mother's a racist over and over.
My beautiful mother's a bigot.
My beautiful mother's pigheaded.
My beautiful mother's not very smart.
My beautiful mother has a black, black heart.

Martin Luther King Poetry Prize, Miami, 2009

BROKEN HUNGARIAN LOVE SONG

In Hungarian the familiar *you* is reserved
for intimate address, otherwise it is *Thou.*

Man on island with tongue.
Man want to love lovingly,
Man wants to make the love,
Cleave to breast, feel bundle of soul.
Fondle, fondle. Dive in,
Burrow under skin. But nicely.
Man no speak native tongue.
Man Friday, Thou Mrs. Robinson.
I no smooth talking man.
Man no feel Thy precise tongue,
Man tongueless, speaks from heart.
Me talk like native American,
Me Kimesaabi, me Tarzan.
Thou very smart. Beautiful Hungarian,
Me go to schule in Cleveland,
No sabe, no literati,
Me Americanischen. Ungaro.
Red blooded kangaroo. Lover-man.

Man want to love lovingly,
Mouth belly, tongue down lily.
Man not eat human flesh,
Not wild boar, not cannibal.
Man like to bore through panty
And eat. Man crazy about belly
And eat. Make the love nicely.

Man die for Thee. Man not get fresh,
Rather die than address
Thou as You. Never You. Never You.

BED BUG

There's a bug in my pajamas
And I can't find it.

If I were a horse I would jerk
My head around
And showing all my teeth
Snap at the gadfly needling
My buttocks.

But I'm a dumb ox.

And the night is a welter of pins.
Fine glass spun into angel hair
Wriggles into the sheets
And the irascible skin.

The morning light
Is a fine drizzle of sand.

And—
There's something I meant to say
But couldn't.

GET WELL CARD

for my neighbor Risto Rundo and for Rosalyn

Even if you don't finish your great work
You will always be remembered
As the most eminent
Octogenarian Serbian-American
Thinker theologian translator
And man of letters

(I see you're not laughing)

I see that lately you are taking
To water and to words
Like a newborn's cry for oxygen
I see you limping in the cage
Of your red-wheeled walker
Regally robed safari helmeted
Inching a lifetime of mornings
Just to reach the water's edge

Your doctor-brother in Berlin
Says there's oxygen in water
Oxygen is everything
So is the word and so is Rosalyn
Who waits with you for the sun to set
But getting back to the word
Your word
As it was in the beginning
And forever shall be yours without end

You've spliced your existence
Between life and letters
Translating Swedenborg and God
Into your native Serbo-Croatian
Submerged as you were with the books
That were your life you'd come up for air
Only now and then—gasping
Your computer was not responding
Brighthouse and Wi-Fi were down again

Here's to you old friend!
A wish you are well again
Well enough to finish
Your grand opus
All the way to the last letter
Of the last word
Of your Apocalypse

ARRHYTHMIA OF INNARDS

A whiskered cat swallowed
A bird whole when a kitten.
Now the meow.
And now the poem

That springs on shoulders,
Shrills ears, shreds sonnets,
The sestina, the double helix,
the DNA spiral. End rhymes

Delayed rhymes.
Delayed ejaculations.

His is an artless GERD,
A throat pregnant with
A fluttering bird.
The heart a twitching

A one-string instrument
Destined to wear itself out.
And that's what this meow
Is all about: Here are his innards.
This is his throat. This is his truth.

LIVING TO KISS THE PAGE

He lives in the lull
Between heart beats.
In dark, silent systoles,
In irritated chambers
Trembling for warmth.

He lives
For the fine tremor
Of waiting lips. But
They are his, so to speak.
To be able to speak.

The murmur
Irrational in muscle only,
Mechanical as the pencil
That skids across the page,
The flutter of eyelids
Between the lines.

The tongue between the lips.

A beat. A miss.

Now the heart is still.
Then suddenly a leap
Toward the mouth.
For the mouth to speak.
For the lips to kiss.

THE FIRST LITTER UNDER STALIN

I was born in *Burok*, not a city so much as a
Hungarian word for *En Caul,* coming out whole
And fully protected in the embryonic sack
Charmed under the star of destiny, although

I found out a few years later that it couldn't save
The litter, four kittens with their eyes glued shut,
Tied into a flour sack, hurled against the wall
By my father, an unemployed judge, who had
Sentenced them to death by blunt trauma.

And they died many deaths sprinkled with the flour
Of our daily bread, and they died not knowing they
Were hurled into a world as hard as it was dark
In the People's Republic of Hungary.

SEEDS

You think my blood
Lighter than it should be.
I have not enough reverence
For the texture of brown earth,
Not the right kind of love
For its deep darkness. My hands
Give me away without calluses.
Only thoughts

In my head: one is a pied brooder,
black and white. It shivers a moment
and gives off a smell.
I look down the throat of the furnace,
A few charred pieces of paper or feathers,
Something dry floats
Out of its mouth. It is August. I want to play soccer,
I want to run.
Your house smells of wheat, millet, poppy seed, lentils.
I saw a tail of a mouse squirm right in. I think
There are more of them. I am not happy diving into
A heap of seeds headlong like into water
Like you thought
I would. What if there's something hidden?
What if I dive in, lose my breath,
And never come back.
If I should sink into that awful sea of seeds piled high
To the ceiling, you would never know how I gave my life.
The roof is a sieve. I breathe seeds. More of them than
Even air. I see nothing else, I think, seeds upon seeds
Upon seeds pour from the apron of the sky.

SELFIE AT SEVENTY ON FACEBOOK

for István a great Hungarian and big brother

Easier to paint a Brillo Pad
Than this scruffy beard
Hot iron the maverick curls
The shorted wires
Of his signature eyebrows
Tone down a wisp of a cowlick
That could keep him
From going Public

And that patchwork nose of his
That would enter rooms
Like the proud prow
Of a Norse galley
If only it could

He is who he is
The face its own canvas
Stone-carved wood
Time carved back to stone
A body of work working the body
Engraving and making
Redeeming its maker

Let it stay roughshod then
Without Photoshop
Hard set in long baked alchemy
By the unbearable heat of paradise

Let this barbarian of the steppes
Wheedle out of all the loveliness
Around him this severe icon of art

But in Florida?
A Russian Christ?

Maybe he ought to smile a little
Just this once for his Profile

Make the rock-faced cheekbones
Stretch the parchment of his skin
And realign the furrowed runes
On his pained attempt at smiling

But under the bristling beard and skin
An ancient bowstring
Is already tightening
So he can grin and bear
The Kodak moment
This time self-inflicted
The twisted smile allowing
An American crown or two
To whiten through

And in that moment
That wink of a camera eye
He squeezes all the life
Out of his likeness
For his Likes

ANNIVERSARY AT BOK TOWER

to my wife of 54 years

We drove all the way from Miami
Only to find the park had just closed
The nice man at the gate let us in

And we had the garden
All to ourselves
All the stillness
And the tower
Girdled with Art Deco flamingos
With all its faux props and circumstance
Measuring time
In slips of honeyed light and shade
In the shutter of a camera eye

There we are
Aglow in the evening sun
Standing stiff as postcards
In this posed photograph
The picture tells only part of the story
Because there was so much more
Because for once I let the moment be

Let it be
Let it be life
And for the moment
Let the light
Make our garden paradise

Let the bells be our clarion call
To all that has been and can be again
Let it be then: the light on your hair
Let it ignite the grass the trees
These darkening leaves

Because nothing no one thing
Not the setting or the rising sun
Can breathe life into moss
As you breathe life into me

And here you are begetting
A fleece of gold and in twilight
And here I am desiring you
Still burnishing
Unmoving but still moved
In this dance of radiance

A HERO'S DEATH

Black leaves shiver in the wind.
The dawn is a glorious red,
I attack with my toy soldiers,
My tanks. I revolve my imaginary
turrets I will die a hero's death.

I throw myself
Into a fascist pillbox,
Grenades tied to my ribs,
I dive like an Olympic champion,
I die like a young Bolshevik.

I will do all this
In the village of Balástya
Where there is a swastika
In the dead center
Of our Persian rug.
Where I am a partisan
Home from Pioneer camp,
A little Judas Iscariot
Who is not scared
To die with a grenade
In his pocket
And pills in his box.

I will die gloriously
For my pioneer comrades.
I will die hatless,
I will die bald headed.

I will die in Siberia
Without sox.
I will die rattle-boned
From exercise and rickets.
I will die an atheist.
I will die deprived of sleep.
My eyes are tired.
Surely my restless legs
Will let me sleep.
I walked all the way
Back to my childhood.
My legs, too, are tired.
Surely they will let me sleep.
I too have promises to keep.

CATS

Are sudden.
Fiercer than jungle smelling,
An oil of brilliant colors,
They're so suddenly large.
Something with the eyes,
Hair bristling several layers of mad.
I wouldn't care for paintings of cats
Arching the spine.
I had a little tiger of childhood,
A bed-warmer son of a bitch
That turned
As I knew it would.
And there's something
About turning.
It is black with streaks
Of silver moving
Through the air
like darts move.
For some time now I have avoided them
Because they are so
Classical.
Even in portraits.
I don't know—
Something happens to kittens
And I associate violence with their
Lovemaking. As the sudden-of-a-wave
They arch
And there is much to this sort of arching.
The same black and silver without warning

Arches. I've seen it in oceans—
Cowering in the corners of kitchens, crazy
To have a fondness for milk
And the smell of liver.
And there's got to be something
About their black rubber tails
Underneath the fur.

LAVABO

Lavabo
With oil
The head first
Bowing in silence;
By the feet, pale acacia blossoms unreal,

And a chalice (a bottle would be vulgar)
Contains the deep velvet drink of the gods.
There is not a ripple either in the air or the wine.

I wash in spring water only.

These walls have not known salted steam.
I will
To the magnificent covers of holy syllables
And translate
In slow motions the texture of God
Into embroidering incense.
Lavabo my meticulous hands.
The many fingers of me.

Awash in the basin is a little fondling.
And that alone
Gives up on the fine lace of vestments
That has since yellowed. The silence can crack
Should anyone cough here
Because the wisdom of alabaster
Needs few words.
Oh I am Pontius

And they outside our light, their throats
Must be dry. Let them.

My palate is olive and honey
Soft.

I am half numb to unclean mouths.

THE CUBIST AND THE IMPRESSIONIST

Taut as the line
Anchoring our craft,
Blocks glimmer
Particulate light
Submerging in chartreuse
A woman's face
In a Picasso geometric.

The sheet as the block
Superimposed, we braid ruefully
Through locks of time,
Twisting angles truer
Than our colored dream,

Because we know such things
Do not exist like swimming
In air or breathing in water,
Except perhaps for her,

Taught to lie on the surface
Splendidly waterlogged
among Monet's water lilies.

LA PALOMA BLANCA

No one will try to reach
Inside the lining, transparent
Especially by the smaller vessels
In rooms smelling of tight rubber
Instead of a cool wind. This is
God's world, the one he made.
I will make a better world.
You won't even know
The colors inside the body.

The top of the head
Runs into a wall,
A princess pirouettes in the hall.

I dream of her.

She is all drama, all fumare,
Retching fire, sometimes air,
A virtuoso in tortuoso,
Her lips exhale feathers
And screams turn into arias.
It is of her music that I dream,
Joywind pouring from the slits
Between her teeth,

White light on her penumbra.
And she sings of love,
Knowing there's no such thing
As the dove coming, still

She would sing *La paloma vendra*
And breathe still
In the snug of the hollow.

CONSPIRING WITH COVID

We are
Biblical lepers
Locked down
By space and time
Abiding to die
Together

Out of air
The panicked heart
Would race
The mare of night
Spur red the skin
Of Dürer withers
Crab of belly
Flick of lizard eyes

The god of chaos presiding
With his lips of lies
Rioters on the Hill
Insurgents in for the kill
Chants of *USA USA*
Hang Mike Pence
Where is Nancy?

A patriot beats a cop
Half to death
With an American flag
A woman with a

Don't Tread On Me flag
Is trampled to death

If this is America
It is the end
The rapture is here
This is where
All conspiracies
Come together

Let us then
Drink to the end
Raise our Bloody Marys
And leave sweaty rings
On the Big Book
There's no Good Book
There is no God

We're fated to lie
Together
Infected forever
In unholy alchemy

We stare dumbly
At the crucifix

We have uncovered
Each other's nakedness
Unmasked lovers
Running a fever
We writhe
On a cross of broomsticks
Hand in hand

We wade across
The River Styx

Wan Rossetti spinsters
Whiskered sisters
Wax women
Of the nickelodeon

We tempt the Tarot
We embalm the Pharaoh
We wither forever
In our arsenic skin

PALMS NURSING HOME

She fed the animals at the zoo last night.
It's better at night, less people, she says,
No lines, and it's pleasantly cool.

So what, you can't see them, you can feel
For them. Shapeless beings with voices
That could tell you many things: the seals have
Asthma, for instance, after a day of trying to please;
How the monkeys touch themselves even in sleep
After a day of taunting bananas. You can hear
Their soughing sighs, and the parrots, too, fly
Off in sweet release, off into colorless dreams
As peaceful as this dark.

No more frightening claps
So gawkers can see their underwings.
No more color. Only the sky is red,
And that from all the exit signs,
Yet it is still safer than the coming of day.

GULFPORT MORNING

with homage to G.M. Hopkins

I found this morning my dominion
My new kingdom of joy awash
In the beatific foam of the tide
My golden dawn's new minion

Poems come to me here
On the wings of seagulls
Sun-dappled as the apple juice
My wife sets on our table

Life is afresh in the golden halo
Of our special time together
Here and everywhere about us
In the whisper of sun-drenched
Palms and white sails

On my holy bike ride
To the Gulfport Library
My brain abuzz with dear
Foolish little things
I will try catching in flight
In my quest for my holy grail
At my desk
On my old laptop

I work here among books
On magical solitary mornings

Their silence my sanctuary
Their solace brooding over me
With warm breasts
And with—ah—bright wings

GHOST TOWN

I'm in your Budapest
Of art nouveux, Bauhaus
And classicist darkness,

Following streetcar cables
To their tortuous tangles,
The smell of snow and ash pits,
The brittle barks of trees,
Skeletons of bareness—
Suddenly you appear
On a windy street—

Corner with gilded, oversized
Headdress. A raging Tai Empress,
A Shiva with many arms and faces,
The tentacles snatching
My spirit to be at one
With the universe of darkness:

Grim icons frozen in aspic,
Faces of porcelain still-lives,
The dark eyes round and vigilant
Promising a cold winter of suffering
And snow-blown shortness of breath.

Tongueless amens to omens of death.

No, there will be no
Color photographs of Budapest

Where the coffeehouses
Are locked on Sunday nights,
Where the grocer mouths his price
From behind bars, where the ice
On the sidewalks is a dangerous
Razor blade, where a ribbed German
Shepherd sniffs at the street
Lamp whose glow is as cold as
The far away moon beyond the clouds.

HALLMARK CARD NO. 1

on my daughter's 50th birthday

Your 50th year is a hallmark year
So I'll give it a shot to be sincere
As grandfather clock goes tick-tock
And your father's heart tachy-tickticktick—
Maybe it's high time to be authentic

True
There were times I've been
An intellectual and emotional bully
And called you names
Not once or twice but many times
Names you'd call a dog—a new puppy
Names like Chooly(sp?)
It was a spontaneous thing
That came on like a tick
And only you and I knew
What it meant—
That maybe I love you truly

HALLMARK CARD NO. 2

on my son's 47th birthday
after the Norman Rockwell plate: First Haircut

Hi Sonny
It's me looking at a picture
Of your first haircut
Your mom says
You wailed like a banshee
But then you sat still
Very still
As if you already knew (before I did)
That life was not a Norman Rockwell
That sometimes you get
Clipped for no reason
Yeah they suck
These rites of passage
From little boy to little man
With polka-dot bow tie and
Hands-in-pocket long pants
Sure you lost your first locks
But accepted the inevitable
With little-man dignity

You've taken some falls but you
Always got up
How many times did you fall
From that unicycle
Before you got the hang of it?
And windsurfing?

You'd go down
And pull yourself out of the water
Sore tired waterlogged
And you'd do this over and over
It's not how you went down
But how you kept getting up
That really got to me

Sometimes I wish I could go
Back in time and do things over
I wish I had been there when they cut
Your hair but I was off somewhere
Chasing ivy laurels or the covers
Of unwritten books imagining them
Being made into a Hollywood movie

Sometimes I wish I could do it over
I mean this fathering thing:
I wish I could've savored every
Little moment with you instead of trying
To make myself over and over
Well—
I just want you to know that whatever
You do wherever you are
You will always be my little guy

MY BROWNING DUTCHESS

Like finest crepe paper,
Poppies are soft
Heart valves. And thin.

Our burning skin
Is a membrane
In that sense.

Flushed, for instance,
When we pout into art,
Brushed aside on a canvas
Or an image penned on a sheet

To force a flower,
Bloom and warm blood
Inside our lining.
To traverse time's
Browning wreath,
When here
We have each other.
And enough love
To outlast verse
So paper thin.

YES I AM GULFPORTIAN!

I am one of many parrots
Squawking my fare of rare rhymes
And lost languages
A mere footnote
An asterisk
Aspiring to be a star
Exploding into Gulfport's fireworks
On the 4th of July
Blossoming and cascading
Into rainbow fountains
Over Boca Ciega Bay

I am young inspired by the old
I am old fired up by the young
They say I'm retired
But I'm re-firing full throttle
As a volunteer bibliophile

I strum my chords under lone pavilions
An artist unabashed to hawk his soul
On paper in clay or papier-mâché
I thumb a ride
On a red-green nostalgia trolley
I ferry lovers of life in space and time
For the magic of Art Walk
On Beach Boulevard

I am more beard than bard
Braying at my bit

To keep the American Dream alive
I am Fire Engine 17
Wailing my siren against time
Blowing my horn and life into lungs
To keep another heart beating
I am Gulfport's Finest
Brothers and sisters in blue
With bright shields
Shielding all regardless of race
Gender or religion

I am a seeker of wisdom
I compose my poems on the pier
Watching the waves crawl
In their silt shimmer
Floating back in time the old dock
That used to be here

I am
A high schooler
Learning our history
In the old museum
In the new award-winning library
I use Wi-Fi to trace my genealogy

I am
A law student at Stetson
A senior citizen taking Tai Chi Chuan
One stylized step at a time
To burst from my cocoon and tango
In the ballroom of our historic Casino

I am
A one-act summer play
A Cathy Award winning director
At the Hickman Theater toasting
Her cast with a glass of rosé
In the iconic Habana Café

I am the O'Maddy's of shipwrecking Margaritas
Stella's breakfast for two and four legged friends
 Pia's for pasta and a taste of Italia
The Neptune and a Literary Afternoon
For feasting on Greek Salad
And a Faustian lecture by Ian O'Hara
And Martha Muzzey on Noam Chomsky's
Bizarre *Hegemony of Survival*

I am the Beach Bazaar
A post office and shop of collectables
It is here I pay my dues
To the Dead Poets Society
By sending out reams of rhyming
Yellowing leaves that die on arrival
So I pick up another book of stamps
And end up buying a Hawaiian shirt
An antique bird cage and a lava lamp

I guess I am
A die-hard hippie in a tie-dye
T-shirt at the Blueberry Patch
High on Jack Kerouac
Bob Dylan and Dylan Thomas

I read my poems in hospices
To give hope to the sick and dying
Who dream of lost porches
And no tomorrows
I teach them to go gently into their
Second birth in the setting sun

I am this earth
This 3.8 square mile plot of land
Where Sabal and Palmetto leaves
Play with the breeze
I am the warm green water
Sunkist pink on the evening bay

I am that humble bungalow
Painted coloring-book teal
With purple geckos leaping
Across my stucco walls
I am an opening in Town Shores
On a finger of water
No longer for sale
Because of a change of heart
By the owner
Because he loves it here
Because he lives writes and loves here
Because he and his wife
Can walk their Augie doggie
In a baby buggy here

There's a saying I am here
Because I am not all there
But at least I know who I am
I am one of the 12,164
Happy to die here

Yes I am
An exotic creature
A snow frog pining for warm dampness
An Alaskan white pelican
An air plant a homeless poet
Dancing to the subterranean beat
Of muffled drums
Shaking the earth to free spirits
From inert bodies
Buried in furrowed barks
And laurel oak

I am three generations
Of spirited Gulfportian women
Who have marched for the right to vote
For equal rights for equal pay
I am an African-American woman
A wounded veteran
Whose artificial limbs propel her
With mechanical grace
In a game of Beach Volleyball

I am a drum circle of proud lesbians
Undiscovered Sapphos and Frida Kahlos
Hearts aglow and beating as one
The sacred thrum of joy ushering in
A new dew-damp dawn

I am a new breed of American
Whose free and unbridled voice
Recharges with new hope
Unafraid to squawk on sidewalks
Mixing harmonizing voices

In church choirs
Readouts and open mics
Bouncing off the Rec Center's
Basketball court
To booming fireworks
Rainbow colors
All voices becoming one
To explode in unison:

Yes I am Gulfportian

EDEMA

In the water she stands
Frogspawn around her ankles
Quietly swelling.
A conch uplifts her
Larger than life, blown hair
Wheezing the sound of the sea.

Wading to her we ask
If she would come to life.
She says she is sad.
Sad as the painting.

Grow vivid, we command.
Catch death of cold like this.
What if your skin
Sucks up all that water.
This is serious,
No longer a game.

I am bloto, she says,
Which means bloated as she
Laughs at the size
Of her thighs
And the prospect of bursting.
She is ashamed of dying
And makes fun.

Were we gods
We would protect her:

Still she would come to life
From frogspawn,
Offering the only substance
Without which she cannot live.
Like pearls they glisten,
We plead for acceptance.
Spawned frogs turn into princes
If you believe.
Your ankles, they are braceleted
If you look at them
A certain way.

A CRUISE THAT NEVER DOCKS

Sea sick and dying
We weather the sea
On an endless cruise
For the aging and dying.
And the guilt abiding.

I dive into a porthole,
You tumble after me,
Shock me in the hold.
"I am old," you say,
"I am old."

You pursue me,
Worm through a hatch,
Hang upside down
And dangle there
For me to catch
Your shrunken head,
The withered hide,
Strands of willow hair,
Every wrinkle, every sore,
My whore of death,
My hour of death.
Abhor. Abhor. Abhor.

PASSING BY THE FREEWAY

Cars swish by without a thought,
I cleave to the weariness of my walk,
Sidestepping pools after the rain.
Nothing is written on them,
Their blistering mirrors
Cower in the darkness

Where the water
Gathers between the cracks.

There's a shopping center
The other side of the overpass,
Its towering columns
Motionless, cold, porous.
The limbs of giants.

Wheels rush past,
Their purpose deliberate,
Almost fixed.

An arm out the window,
Another gripping the wheel.

The mall is abandoned.
The Spartan Department Store's
Windows boarded up,
Glass, gravel, chunks of rubber
Litter the parking lot.
The weeds have grown tall,

The smell of skunk
Like concord grapes.

I think of the animal's carcass,

Cars pass,
I pass,
This too shall pass.

HEART OF STONE

Fine hairs feather,
Scale, shingle in time,
Fibrous from ankle
To waist, callous in stone.
Still the likeness must be
One of fleeting stance,
Nimble feet taking root,
Impossible to totter
In a sea of dust.

Behold the pyramids rising
Out of the dance of dunes,
Hardened banyan roots
Like sclerotic arteries
Snaking in and out of stone.
And the strands of Gizeh's
Hair: how the builders
Looked up, astounded

Or Galatea's unyielding lips,
Enchanted. How the sculptor
Feared the coming of her
To life: the loss of grace,
The creaking joints lurching
Forward those mechanical arms.

THE PIETÀ

Is guarded behind glass
Ever since a Hungarian madman
Took a hammer to the Holy Mother
And to the overgrown, bearded baby
In her lap.

I see clearly now why
that invisible wall
had to be between us,
how you lost your first born
who poisoned himself as a toddler,
how his small thrashing body
must've grown limp in your hand.

How artfully we've been swaddled
in marble hardness since then.
How we have kept our distance,
as if loving once were enough,
as if dying once were enough,

as if one poem were enough
from these poems to burn,
for both of us to rest in peace,
fully grown now, marble heavy
in this paper urn of forgiveness.

THE OWL

for Larry Donovan

Ruff of feathers, night
Watchman of gardens,
Ancient gruff
Of bearded grandmothers,

Sire of poems for time
Eternity. Make me wise,
O widening eyes, wise enough
To know my destiny.

Ire of nighthawks,
Preying goatsuckers,
Give me a beak sharp enough
To peck at stars,

Duller plumage to blend with day,
Duller vision of all that risks
Shrinking stars to asterisks.

A POEM IN A PANDEMIC

A poem
Is not it
Or is it?
What is?
Milkshakes
To go,
Straws
Hermetically
Sealed
In paper,
Chocolate
For me,
Vanilla
For her.
We sip
Our shakes
Forehead
To forehead
As we did
Half a century
Ago.
We laugh
At the
Unbearable
Lightness
Of being,
No longer
Worried
About

Clogging
Arteries,
Ahh—
Two straws
Slurping
The sweet
Infusion
Of joy.
We are
High risk
And we
Know it.
This is it.
This is
What we
Do in a
Pandemic.
One cough
And it's
Covid.
We're
Positive.
And laugh
Till we're
Red in the
Face.
Life couldn't
Be better!
If one
Gets sick,
The other
Gets sick.
We will die

Together
Hermetically
Sealed
Like the
Masks
Hanging
Inside
Our door
And the
Big box of
Nutrasystem
Waiting
Outside
Too heavy
To lift.

GULFPORT PIER

How the frayed waves crawl
Redundant in their silt shimmer
To float back the old floating dock
That used to be there

Across today's O'Maddy's
Defrocked of history in blue
And yellow Day-Glo colors

Still the murky water swells true
To the arthritic roots of mangroves
Awash in the eternal lapping

Each barnacle creating
Antiquity anew in its own time
In its own sharp braille of time

It too could narrate the history
Of Boca Ciega Bay
Restless under the new
Factory-treated wood
And pointing a finger at our age
Ringed all about by droll aluminum

VARIATIONS ON LOCKDOWN

I
I see my wife in Technicolor
Her fingers are making
Digital angels
And in high resolution
The large eyes close in
On each other
In ever-widening circles
The blooming retinas of owls
Wings the pandemonium of parrots
Look at her working
She is creating
She is rendering
In lockdown
More radiant than her screen
She glows like a mother to be
But her being blooming positive
Is less than contagious
For her the virus is
As it is
She is right
Where she should be

II
I envy her
I'm locked on to YouTube
K-9 vehicular extractions in particular
Violent police chases in Los Angeles
That is as close as I get

To angels in high def
People I avoid like the plague
It is my plague
One cough and I'm positive
The omen a murder of crows
Naked and afraid
I am wide-eyed and contagious
Insist my wife keep me company
As I watch dogs
Hunt down shirtless subjects
Who cough on cops in masks
She pretends not to hear me
It is what it is
And in HD
We are right
Where we should be

OPENING AT TOWN SHORES

From a drone
The man-made waterways
Spread out like fingers

A sailboat sputters
Past humdrum condominiums
Toward the mouth
Of Boca Ciega Bay

The old Mercury engine
Puffs popcorn clouds
Before it stalls
Then a lull

The timing near perfect:
The wind billows the sails
Full sail ahead
The ageless current
That drives the air
That stirs the water
And moves the hull
Toward the sea moves me
And causes my fingers
To move across the page

The drone zooms in to showcase the pool
As it juts into a widening channel
The area deserted
Except for an old man near the water's edge

He is regally robed and safari helmeted
Sitting and writing
In the cage of his red-wheeled walker

It is summer in Florida

He interrupts himself to look around
Then goes back to taking notes
On the secret life of plants
Zoom in closer:
I am that man

I open myself to the silence
There's enough of it here
To hear the tiniest of wings
Not the drone taking
Wing from MacDill Air Base
But the sound of a frail creature
Swollen with pollen
Toiling to hold itself up
In the empty air
Waiting with grace
For the fall

The inevitable splash

In that same instant
Sun sparklers trawl their nets
Across the surface
To catch this quiet
How could I have missed it?
Something sacred was about to land

Swimmers invade the pool
Instead of swimming they stand
In the water or move a limb
Talk of tai chi and yoga
And cancer and catheters
A father with Alzheimer's
A neighbor's lingering terminal illness

A death

For a few seconds all is quiet
Maybe too quiet
The air begins to cloy
With baby oil and iodine
A professor whose gray hair is braided
Announces that the spirit
Must be grounded in light
Another interrupts her
With *The Power of Now*
Soon all is aflutter
The sounds distant and nonsensical
As the chirping of birds

What they leave behind
Is stillness so maddening
The shrill lawnmower
Is welcome noise
Stillness then
Is not the absence of sound
And loveliness not always a flower
Unless I see it for the first time
How the filaments in the center
Thinner than paper

Aspire upward
Opening
Never preening
And when its time has come
A petal does not mind drying
Never minds
Falling

Under the nose
Of a mechanical owl
And barrier fishing lines
Two Florida sparrows land
To gulp water
Splash one another
And spur the moment to frolic
One flies away
The other looks on
The slight wings beating the water
To drown its sorrow
Before it too flies off
In the same direction

Stillness is not
Always the lack of motion
The birds were not nervous
When they gave themselves
Over to doing what they do
They have flown beyond artificial nets
Even ceremonial doves
Defy formation without
Fretting about falling
Or bettering their last
Audition

On the Tiki hut
A palm frond loses its footing
The vertical drop
Fans into a swan dive
Still it misses the water
And scrapes along the pool's edge
Waiting to be airborne again

In the shadow
Of a sundial
A caterpillar plant comes to life
Breakdancing to a sudden gust
The stem shivers and little hairs
Thin and fall
Into transparence
In the whitening sun
Each floats on air
To its own rhythm
Its own
Stylized breaking crawl

The mower cuts all that have landed
In its path into finer filigree
To be airlifted or sprayed
Into green water
And carried out colorless
As they reach the sea

They are as much a part of the great
Current as the dancing seahorse
The feather star
Or the rainbow anemone
What was dander in the grass

Is now a great spirit
More brilliant in its sheerness
Than the oleander

The pool light comes on underwater
I watch the lightshow on the bottom
Lace curtains dance in and out of focus
And shudder at the slightest touch

A single breath from me sets off ripples
Changing the mesh of an entire universe
Each pattern more intricate than the last
As sound waves translate
Into shape-shifting
Fractals of light

I keep blowing on the surface
Mesmerized by zebras crawling
Down my leg
The shifting lines continue to drill
Their spiraling illusions
Right through the concrete
To the underside of life

All I do is to poke
A finger in the water and—voila!
A diaphanous *mandala*
Alive and billowing
Spreads out and downward
And starts to gel
In the viscous slow motion
Of a lava lamp overflowing
To an underground river

And an endless formless
Waxen ocean

 The submarine light
Insinuates itself through
The murky green of night vision
Into the very treacle of the sea
And what unfolds before the eye
Is an undulating breathing
Undiscovered yet familiar
—opening—
Forming and reforming
In fleeting time-lapse
Corals becoming reefs becoming
An island of coral
The runway of the landing

As I tread way
Into the secret life of the jungle
Leaves waver

Dry and yellow
Into haystacks of old Europe
Changing in shape and color
Into towers of Cholla cactuses
Teepee huts crowned with
The feathers of raised spirits
Images of burial mounds
Subterranean pyramids

Glowing embers red and volcanic
Burst and spatter
Every edifice cornice and porous

Surface of concrete jungle
With a riotous magma of color
Melting and molding
Every molecule
Into sacred geometry

Gecko gargoyles mechanical owls
A razor-sharp sunburst
Appear in glaring colors
To scare off buzzards unwanted
Solicitors and all other bloodsuckers
That impersonate time

From the Kenmore to Embassy row
Condominiums raise
Their sacred totems
To the beat of Tocobaga drums
An ancient wind instrument
Billows the sails
And makes the fingers of water tremble
Artists bricklayers dragon slayers
Sailors and whistling minstrels
Woman warriors
Weary from battles for their
Own secret heart
Every grain of sand
Blown here from distant shores
Every brush and crush of petal
Filament of flower sundial and owl
An animate and timeless
Sacrament of grace

THE ART OF TAXIDERMY

Look for a blackbird flitting on the wire
Thinking it to be a branch. Its coat, almost
Blue, will glint a black angel toward heaven
Before sparks singe the metallic beak
And breathe from it an animal smell.
It is to die despite the shining.

Take the worm from the mouth
And lop off the starry comb,
Tossing the innards
To a whiskered cat. Inflate
With air until the bird is full
And clouds sail by. Cool. Spread
Fine-needle frost to the wings.

Air bloats skin
If made to swallow.
Wait until the heart is still
Or not there at all—

Then stuff it with the stars of night
The unvacuumed night of stars
Take care not to stretch the arsenic
Skin. And when the green and marble
Eyes, cooler than glass, light up the self-
Illuminating body, it is time.
When eyes flicker into glowworm,
It is time to serve the body.